My Diverse Manic Freeways Of Thoughts

Kenya McGhee

authorHOUSE®

AuthorHouse™
1663 Liberty Drive
Bloomington, IN 47403
www.authorhouse.com
Phone: 833-262-8899

Published by AuthorHouse 01/19/2023

ISBN: 978-1-7283-7790-2 (sc)
ISBN: 978-1-7283-7788-9 (hc)
ISBN: 978-1-7283-7789-6 (e)

Library of Congress Control Number: 2023901089

Contents

About the Author vii

Prologue xi

"The Shedding of our Skin" 1

"Poetically Me" 3

"My Temporary Abode" 5

"New Life" 6

These Times 8

Heavenly Distractions 10

"Priceless Me" 12

"Jails, Institutions And Death" 14

"Mental Control" 16

"Choices" 18

"Scars And Wounds" 19

"Broken Home" 20

"My Second Son" 21

"Lonely child" 23

"Since I Dont Now You Like That" 25

"Young Seva" 27

"A Mothers Need" 29

The Main Ingredient 31

"G" 33

"Prize winner" 35

"Master Piece" 36

"Inner Child" 38

"Colors" 39

"Leave me alone" 41

Love Trapped 43

"Victim to Victor" 45

"Goals" 47

"The River That Runs" 48

"You Made Me New" 50

"Greater Is Coming" 52

"Green Light" 54

"Innocent Seeds" 56

"You Cant Win With Sin" 58

"Street Life" 60

"Bullet Magnets" 62

"Gang Involvement" 64

"Emotional Thug" 66

A Better Place Now 68

"Fast Food Franchise" 70

"Mature Intimate Connections" 71

"You Love Me You Want Me" 73

"When Love Hurts" 75

"How Am I Suppose To Love Again" 76

"Fall" 78

"Escape" 80

Hood Love 82

Idle confinement 84

The Penal System 86

"Deface" 88

Epilogue 91

About the Author

I was born in September of 1974 in a small impoverished city up north Toledo, Ohio. Born with no character only identity I was soon shaped and molded into what my upbringing and culture had embedded in me throughout my molding process. Living in a city with an environmental magnet to a variety of strongholds I became exposed to drugs, gangs, hustling, which landed me in my darkest valley. My reserved destination of incarceration. Grateful of it not being the grave I had a fresh awakening as I transformed into my new unfamiliar identity. I was gifted beauty for ashes. I began to express my self through my writing. My poems are derived from my inner emotions and thoughts articulated to convey my life journey of how I've overcame my complex past and got presented these wings to fly and soar over these prison walls. I have developed the strenght to persevere on despite my past or present circumstances. With the ability to step out of my normal comfort zone and reach out for more new positive avenues to explore in my remaining lifetime here on earth. To leave my children and grandchildren with not just a prison number but a profound empowering legacy that will stand as an imprint in their lives throughout their lifetime. As a mother of five I present to you a portion of my diverse manic freeways of thoughts.

This book is dedicated to the entire McGhee family. My mother Christine McGhee and my late father Robert M. McGhee. My sibling Corey, Mickey McGhee, Ashantia McGhee-Jones and most of all my five innocent seeds my children Destiany Spencer, Dynasty, Michael Jr., Misan Darden and Mateo Betancourth. Its never to late to rectify your bad choices of detours in life. As long as you have the breath reach.

A special thanks goes out to my Recovery mentor Ms. Duncan-Alexander for her many flourishing seeds of transforming deposits into my life.

Blessing and love to my three angels my grandchildren Sy'Aire, Sy'cere Carter and Kali Darden.

Prologue

As I sojourn on in my journey of life I sit in a prison cell with an album full of memories of my past and present days. The good and bad times of my life. Thinking of how quick time elapse and how over time things come back around full circle in so many ways in life. Something I never really took the time to sit still and pay attention too. Ive always heard the statement "life is short" and now I truely understand and feel the meaning of it. To short to waste any of it. As we proceed through out this life on earth. The only instructions Ive found essential that has provided me creation was Gods word. Peace contentment and discernment has been my greatest increase. My past journey before my incarceration was ultimately aspired and driven to increase my currency and provide for my family how ever I could no matter the risks or consequences behind it. I knew of my risks but never took heed of my consequences or even cared. It was my mission, my life, my normalized conduct. That had shaped and molded me in so many ways my mind and eyes could see no different. It was my way or the highway. And with that one track mindset I found myself confined to Daytons corrections on a fifthteen year prison sentence for arson and two involuntary manslaughter charges. One being the death of my codefendant, my own father. Receptive, accountable and very remorseful for my actions. I collect my thoughts of all my left turns in my past trying to pinpoint where did things go wrong in my life and how did I get to this point of my life. The times of my diversions onto the wrong roads that has hindered my successes in life. Bad choices unhealthy relations, toxic substances taking me off the path of my

dreams and goals. I cant help but wonder where I would have been if I wouldnt have took those detours. I can also recognize all the blessing that was bestowed on me back then. How God provided, protected and gave me chance after chance. Opened door after door of opportunities placing me in several positions to win and prosper in life. At that moment my eyes or mind couldnt grasp on to that. I couldnt see, hear or understand. But the true glory of it all is that I been through the fire and again I state "through" without any damage. Only a new restored body of much more value and purpose. Realizing that it doesn't matter how you start off in life or where you are its all about how you finish your race. And for all the people who have struggled and failed in life use that experience to discover your strengths. There's lessons through out it all providing us wisdom, provision preparation and guidance for our future. It becomes our testimony in life, our then to now, our before and after, our death to life. The shedding of our skin, our metamorphosis that transforms us to our new creation. No longer will I let my struggles or failures have anchors on me in a way that weighs me down into self-pity keeping me stagnant in life. I can now embrace my past and use it as a tool an opportunity to teach me of how I need to live and what direction I need to take navigating on through life. Through out the rest of my destination here on earth. Remaining focused with the strengths cultivated through my resiliency. I can now use my anchors as empowerment not only for myself but for others conveying my story of how Ive overcame my struggles and pain through out my journey.

R.evised
E.nhanced
A.ctions
C.hanging
H.ardships

Simmering in my own self-pity of a variety of past issues. I became my own physician, therapist and teacher. Running through my journey filling all my vacancies the best way I felt was suitable for me. Lacking insight and knowledge I self-medicated engaged in unhealthy

relations and was driven by criminal thinking I was living stagnant after the descension to my darkest valley. I slid off of my slippery slope comfortable stuck in my created mess. I was held hostage for quite a while. Actually a huge portion of my life. The obstacles of trauma, strongholds and pain eventually led me to my depleted desparate state. And during that time I found myself receiving a fifthteen year prison sentence. Over those years I had an awakening coming to the realization that with out a reach for the proper help everything will always remain the same or only get worse. And the only way to begin my life sustaining transformation was for me to be willing to accept the proper help and surrender my old behaviors and reach for the change. By revised enhanced actions changing hardships. I had to self-examine myself and my situations by revising my thinking and actions due to my circumstances and afflictions. I had to enhance my actions with a greater driving effort to change. Stepping out of my normal comfort zone as I chauffeured myself to explore new enlightening paths through my hardships. I discovered that it had transitioned me into another state of renowed thinking and identity by the "Shedding of my skin" Today I recognize that without my efforts to reach I would have remained the same individual simmering in my issues & old ways similar to a dog running in circles chasing its own tail. A never ending cycle comfortable in my own meaningless state. When all it required was an R.E.A.C.H.

"The Shedding of our Skin"

I am writing about the transition from lost now found,
Darkness to light, one being into another, death to life,
Old skin to new skin.
Its like the rejuvenation of skin
The restoring of flesh over flesh of an open wound
And that does not happen all at once but over a duration of time.
Little by little not specific, but unpredictable start to finish.
My skin was tough, tough as leather
It had to be broken in, sat and stomped on over time
It was miss-used, abused
Unappreciated, contaminated and unpurified with uncleanliness toxic
substances, people, places and things.
Miss-guided with ill desires and will
But by grace my transformation had begun
Before it was to late there was a death to life ending activated
In my darkest space, In my mess
The shedding of my skin had begun
There was a shift in my ways my desires my walk and talk
My mind and heart had started to align up with the whispers of Gods
divine word.
My old skin of the one-track roads, addictions, attitudes and desires.
I no longer craved or desired
My mouth was filled with affirming empowerment for myself and
others.

I was able to articulate the things I felt, thought, wanted and needed, liked and disliked.

Speaking fluent in the moments with no more hesitation or reluctancy holding my words or fear.

I am shedding my broken past of my childhood strongholds and obstacles.

Letting go of my resentments and anything that has kept me in chains.

Ive moved from complacentcy to contentment with a peace and understanding I cant explain.

Compelled to be of service and good works with a drive of passion energy and love.

I AM SHEDDING

No longer stagnant in my engrafted past

Now free and flying through the fog, trauma and strongholds that once hindered me and my growth in so many ways.

Today my mind is renewed with thoughts and visions of life and light.

My new skin enables me to persevere on in faith and hope.

Trusting and dreaming of an abundant life sober and free

To properly handle and face life gratefully

Overcoming any of its obstacles that may come up against me

I am shedding with new profound revelations and abilities

My shedding has provided me with a variety of new talents and gifts.

Something that my old skin would have never allowed....

Continuing to shed "The Shedding of my Skin"

"Poetically Me"

My poems are my interior notes of the thoughts I quote
My mental emotions and stories that's held within
Transferred onto journals from scribing with this paper and pen

My poems are the words that are heard in my comatosed sleep when
Im in bed after hours
Or my formulated thoughts that arrive in the shower
And seemingly awkwardly to say that they derive from the running
water

My poems are birthed out of the sounds and wounds of this loaded
strapped soul
With the inside words thats trapped awaiting to therapeutically unfold
and be told
With similar relatable hints of my true life journey events
To stimulate your mind
Lift you up and replace you in a new destination of my time
Chauffeuring you on a captivating sensational journey
Driving keeping you interested so you could never feel bored or lonely

My poems are my surmountable diverse imagination of manic thoughts
Untamably chasing and evading one another from being caught
Flowing wild and free for no specific reason
Exposing you to a variety of topics
Capable of springing you from season to season

My poems assist my mind to stablely direct and land my feet
Expand my horizon and envision the foreign places thats out of my reach
It aids to my education my search beliefs and also the words that I speak

My poems are poetically me expressing myself so beautifully
Revealing and extracting out all of the toxic contaminants that has been exposed and engrafted inside of me.

"MY POEMS ARE POETICALLY ME"

"My Temporary Abode"

My temporary abode was my darkest hole.
Till the light broke through the bricks illuminating my soul,
Brighter than any gold.

Exhaustion had began to devour me while I was running through this
prison time.
Then the angels appeared lifting me up assuring me that I'll be just fine.
Resuscitating my life, saving me from my despair.
Whispering in my ear, child please know that I have never left you
alone.
I've always been there.

My thoughts and weaknesses were screaming enough is enough.
But God said when I am weak, I am strong.
So let the rough cultivate the tough.

Now I'm fortified full of vitality standing tall.
Overcoming it all.
Although my body still sits behind these steele gates.
My mindset and soul is free flying over these prison walls.

"New Life"

according to the power that worketh within you

I was the streets bait
The hustles mate
And my addictions degrade
Now #89451 Im writing, reading and flipping through my own book
of life pages
Although withholding my dreams and goals that had never left my side
This robust heart for my family was my concrete reason to provide
It was the instant thrill & pleasure from fast money and renowned
hood fame
Everyone from Toledo to Houston had grown to know my name
Now its the prison systems checkmate
While I sit in a cell behind these steele gates
Praying for a redo, eagerly anticipating my date
Presently taking this time to evolve and resolve my past old perspectives
Today I have a renewed mindset and all my choices are now selective
Looking through clearer lenses with new visions at bay
With God all things are new and he provides the light that paves my way
And suddenly all my past character defects are fading away
Go on ahead and go astray
Allow me to continue to shed my skin and walk into this new being
Hello new day
Transformation is the only choice to win

And finally that is what I am now seeing
An unfamiliar refined identity I could have never foreseen

Out of the darkness and into the light
My worth could never again be demeaned
Hello New Life.....

These Times

These times universively we cant seem to agree on a proper worldly solution
It has come down to these perilous times
Where no one is fine and the enemy is stealing souls at the drop of a dime
Unable to handle emotions or conflict unreasonable judgements of violence are being made
Resulting to guns for solutions
Retorting to criminal activities extending this negative earthly pollution

Everyone is wishing to change something
Whether its their gender or origin birth name
Were no longer at peace with our creators mold
So untamably the prevelance of cosmetic surgery is being sold
So we alter our bodily appearance to rejuvenate our youthful soul

Some wish to magically back track
Only to retrieve their pure intact youth back
Reflecting on their past in hopes to recast
Grasp on to and make it last

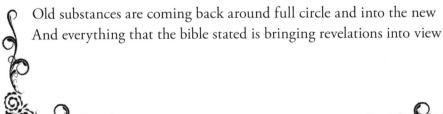

Old substances are coming back around full circle and into the new
And everything that the bible stated is bringing revelations into view

These times the children dont play or stay young under the invigorating sun

The newfangled technology and social media has got them all sprun

The economies global air we breathe no longer appears sheer its polluted

While the unfortunate worldwide racism for some is satisfying and everlastingly suited

Its time that we unite in love

Exclude the guns and move away from the center of this wasteland

Remember who is king

Follow his instructions and plans

That he has set for us as we reside on this temporary secular land

Heavenly Distractions

Heavenly distractions Gods divine guidance that will set you in an idle space of quietness
Away from all the noxious noise
Where you are only able to hear his voice commands and promises
Instilling in us that indescribable peaceful poise

Heavenly distractions a time when your will is contending with Gods will
Your tongue thoughts and actions are being renewed by an alteration of changes on a consistent basis
Elevating our skills

Heavenly distractions feeling of conviction when our actions are not of him
Condemning our hearts towards his truth and glory
While shining his light to lead the way
Abling us to stand firm and upright in confidence
Boldly persevering on to spread his story

Heavenly distractions provides us elation and joy in our most disoriented discorded times
A comforter and friend through the most loneliest coldest dark nights
Appearing as an illuminating light that revises our sight

Heavenly distractions showers us with rain meeting our every need with floods of the greatest first love that fortifys and elevates us to new levels with supernatural powers
Revealing us with talents and gifts of our hidden unfamiliar abilities
Awakening us with a newly birthed life

Heavenly distractions intervenes in our life at our lowest pits of defeat
Compelling us to surrender and seek his counsel
Which ascends us to higher limits of hope
Strengthening us to annihilate and overcome any battle or failure

Heavenly distractions
The wisdom and assurance we receive that ignites the transformation of our old mindsets to teardown to reframe and rebuild on a more robust foundation

Heavenly distractions turns your sins into wins
Opening up new perspectives renewing our minds
Like the Shedding of our skin
Putting our old negative flesh and past to and end

Heavenly distractions is like Gods mother nature sending blowing winds and snow storms down on a busy families home
Interrupting their regular routine
Blocking them in so they can spend quality time with one another and no ones left alone

Heavenly distractions intervenes and uplift your predetermined plans

With different directions
Rerouted heavenly destinations
Designed for upper levels of increase
Surpassing you from where you previously had settled and made plans to be

Those Heavenly Distractions

"Priceless Me"

Satan, Im priceless you cant put that price on me
This beautiful structure GOD has created simply does not have a fee
So all that you proclaim to offer theres no need you see
I can send up all my requests and receive them by getting down on bended knees
As I reflect back on my past when everything about me was a fee
And my entire mentality was driven by nothing but currency
I rendered you my soul
And just then my whole life had took its toll
I started chasing and lusting wealth
Which had become so detrimental to my health

I lost all my sense of reasoning my direction, visions and goals I was no longer seeing
I was brought with a pricetag on my head
But realistically I was living as the dead
When my sole purpose was to benefit the family I once led
Eventually you would place a huge dent in me
Incarceration has found me and grief surrounds me

As your merchandise and due to your purchase I allowed you to depreciate my value
You were persistently attracting, while consistently attacking
But know I landed back in my original owners hands, who initially gave me life

With instructions for no strife
New birth, My worth
Recognizing all that he created me to be without a price or a fee
Your wicked ramifications that had once followed
Mournfully, tormented me my family and friends suffering is what we
had swallowed

And as your merchandise
I still had to pay my own price
While your plans were to dismantle, distract and corrupt
Here I sit stuck in the prison system on my but
Satan, I have just a few more words "IM PRICELESS"
I cant be bought thats the lesson that I was taught
No longer am I living in hell because my soul is not for sell
No longer a commodity my merchant is now GOD
And he is who embodies me

"PRICELESS ME"

(Mark 8:36) And how does a man benefit if he gains the whole world
and loses his soul in the process?

"Jails, Institutions And Death"

Powerless addictions are leading us through many tests
Keeping us entangled in bondage, relentlessly running through time
Neglecting our health and avoiding our mental rest
While we surf on the clouds
Floating so high in the sky we lose sight of our first origin at birth
We begin to diminish and self sabotage our self worth
As we continue to travel further and further away from this secular earth
Was it better for me to fall from the clouds and end up in jail
Get rehabilitated to restart my lifes journey
And get presented these wings to soar & sail

The mental institutions wont release us on bail
You become the states experimental inmate they claim to stabilize in jail
Their clinicians posing as magicians
Contaminating our bodies with more toxic drugs
Causing us more elevated health conditions
That's their tradition
Educated to stabilize and numb our issues
Administering us more dope in medical syringes
Poking them in our epidermal tissues
Now grateful, clean and sober given once again another chance

Blessed to have overcame and escape death
This time I commit to put forth my best
And leave everything else up to God to handle the rest
Drugs leading to jails, institutions and death.

"Mental Control"

In my adolescence days I started partying to be cool
Engaging into negative relations and situations even dropping out of school
Later on down the line it escalated I self-medicated
Impaired ingesting more potent toxic substances
Which directed me straight to this position to lose
I suffered a tremendous amount of consequences
I was running my race through life staging my own set of rules
Throughout my journey I encountered a vast amount of teachers
But they could never captivate my attention for my lessons at school
Because I concealed a sporadic attention span
That was always bouncing and running wild
Similar to the pesky traveling grass hopping locust
Due to my complex corrupted disconnected mental wires
It was severely difficult for me to gain control of my focus
My entire life I carried this component with a wide range of racing thoughts
Flowing with diverse speeding freeways jumping lane to lane
Trying to escape one another and ellude from being caught
Instead of looking at it as a hindering mental illness disability
I had to gain control and chauffeur my seclusive thoughts
Gather and consider the content putting it all in perspective
Appoint them as powerful tools
And lay out my own open choice of directives
Which seemingly turned up and appeared to be totally impressive

Reflecting back in my past I lost control
I use to rely on the toxic substances to barricade those speeding roads
But over my sobriety awakening years I realized that they were not permanently blocked but only froze

And as the substance faded I was ignorant dumbfounded to the fact that they were only numbed
I ended up finding myself right back at square one
As they defrost I embarked on another mental cycle of chasing all my diverse speeding thoughts
Once again they all arose
But living life today Ive gained authority of my MENTAL CONTROL

"Choices"

We are not aware or certain about the multitude of daily choices we have to endure each day.
Is it this way or that way, should I agree or disagree
Ive learned that contemplation should come prior to any action
Before we become to encounter any of lifes embarking pressure
That most of the time leads us to a wide range of negative sudden impulse reactions
Which succeedingly causes us a lifetime of damage

Which opens up the strain
But then what paths do we take to release the pain
The various options we choose to tame the brain
And its never ending process of thoughts
Like the turbulence of rain

The clinicians, physicians posing as the magicians claiming to calm the mental strain
The measureless roads we choose to maintain
That only usually momentarily numbs the pain
Delusively paralyzing our physical mental sensations
Unabling us to face the reality of this simple plan of our predestination
To our heavenly location

Were in need of those heavenly voices
before we make our daily choices.

"Scars And Wounds"

Scars and wounds embedded externally and internally
Over my body and throughout my soul
Authenticating me into my natural being
Causing so much pain and pleasure
As I look into this reflection in the mirror
Its the transformation of this person I am visually seeing

Scars and wounds
Its the gain from the pain
Its the pleasure causing great deals of measure
I could be licking my wounds wearing them proudly as badges, my
stripes of honor
To remind and motivate me on futher away from this life I left behind me
Or I can continue to bleed staying stagnant in my past
Which vainly amounts to nothing and I will never last

I'll just be repeeling the scabs to relive and resurface the bloody trauma
of the pain I once had

Continuously reflecting leaving me in my mess, feeling depressed
Or I can just move on ahead and considerate as one of life experienced tests

Nevertheless Im grateful to remain sane, living and blessed
Im leaving it all up to "GOD" to handle the rest

SCARS AND WOUNDS

"Broken Home"

The broken home windows are displayed with smog
From the pain of the roaming lost souls suffocating gasp of breaths
Lamenting over its deficiency
Every creak from the floor footsteps speaks the language of a story to
be exposed
While the lost souls roam throughout the home
Carrying around a facade of impressions of fake smiles
Operating in mechanical mode
The heightened level filled trauma consumes every room and flows over
the walls
As the covering hand shuts the mouth
Sweeping the dirt under the carpet from the family brawl
Theres a clock on the wall thats stopped dead in its tracks
It wont return back to its normal functions
Until it regains its distant lineage back
The hearts are cold, The dysfunction is growing old
Every door is locked barricading emotions
Inclining them to be stuck stopped in its surfacing spot
Dimishing the self-sufficiency of pride
Imprisoned debating with my conscious if I should chose to stay alive
The conditions inside the home has become exacerbating
Whereas the structure of the home is overwhelmingly deteriorating

"My Second Son"

My third seed
was my child with asthmatic needs
He had big bright eyes
and Braids split down the center of his heads with beads.

He was my little shorty crunch
my heart
out of the bunch
Who use to sit up in his highchair and rock left to right side
to side for his lunch.

Loving to spend his free time playing video games
and has always curiously aimed for fame
Jumping into Lil Troys studio in the garage in MoCity.Tx
trying to create a rap name.

Later living life for fun
consuming toxic substances, found incarceration, was walking the
streets toting a gun.
My Second Son
Mommy just want you to know
that it takes time to grow
So sit still and think a while and try to slow your roll.

You must put God first in your life and you'll be fine
doors will abruptly open
and your patient will soon start to blossom with time.

"MY SECOND SON"

"Lonely child"

Dwelling under this roof that use to be bullet proof
I sit out here lost home alone
With visions of you that I carry when you were still at home
I await daily to feel your love over the discourse we have on the phone
This house remains vacant
And the fresh smelled aroma from you washing our laundry still lingers
throughout the vents
Coming up from the basement
And the walls still echoe your consoling voice
After the authorities came in and abducted you surviving standing alone
has been my only choice
Im a lonely child
Your 1 out of 5 children with adopted emotions of an only child
And when they sentenced you to fifthteen years in prison my entire
world turned wild
Im still your big bright eyed child only subtract the smile
Because when these floors get to creaking your footsteps it questions me
was your crime really worth the while
I envision you in the kitchen, in my bedroom planting kisses in my sleep
Awakening me to late walmart runs
Say'n son come grab a videogame its gonna be fun
You ten years in now we walking down them miles
You stated Son hindsight is always better than foresight
And if I was thinking rational and sober it wouldnt had resulted to this
and Ill redo that night

I should have been grateful and appreciated all that I had
And if I retained the knowledge I hold today
You wouldnt be displaying those perplexed frowns living sad
Maybe then Ill still have the presence humor of my dad

Lonely child, Its almost over now
I just pray the vacant structure is still standing
And the resentment of destruction hasnt torn it completely down
Have faith in God
He promised to restore back what we lost 10 fold
I understand your cold
And for me to keep telling you Im coming home each year is getting old
But trust God and find strength
Ill be back home and things will come back around
We will renovate that home
And it will be the best in town
You wont be left alone
And we will no longer have to express our love over this phone
The flood of your tears will reduce from being spilled
And all of your empty vacancies will then be filled
Then you wont be lonely
Sitting listening to the noises of the broken home
I left behind that crys and moans

"Since I Dont Now You Like That"

Since I dont know you like that
I do know your loyal and have my first sons back

I know you stayed down with him riding on them rocky waves through
deep water
Keeping his head afloat and not jumping off the boat

Since I dont know you like that
I know throughout his darkest days you conceived his child
A new extension to our family "Kali" a beautiful baby girl
That keeping him focused working remaining in the house not in the
streets running wild

Shes currently shining the light in yall world
Giving my son a purpose in life
Praying youll remain and continue on and eventually become his wife

I know that your home stay clean and you not living trife
Keeping my son belly full resembling a part of my life

I know thay you polished but still wont take no shit
And if you get pissed off you would go in the kitchen and grab a knife
and be ready to hit

I also feel that you dont be on no other niggas dxxk
Because I know you know where you at is it

Since I dont know you like that
I just keep my mouth shut and sit
But just keep on thinking that I dont know shxt

"Young Seva"

My last bae
And if I could do it all again
I would hold you so close to my heart throughout all of my days

Its so much I wanna show you
Only me and God knows the extent of how bad I want to hold you
I dont know if I told you

I wish I could erase and take on all of your pain
Sometimes just the thought of you hurting will drive me insane
But just by me hearing your voice over the phone and seeing you smile
on your photos momentarily some what eases my strain

I want you to please understand and know that even though Im away
that my love is still here and will always remain the same

We have better days coming ahead
So be strong and courageous and continue to always hold up your head

Your my last and final seed
My unique Columbian son with the heart shaped birthmark planted
on the side of your head

I admire your strengths continue to stay focused
And fed from the promises our almighty God has spoken
Trusting and believing that you are one of the chosen

"A Mothers Need"

You are the sunlight of my day that shines
Reminding me of the strengths you've gained
From all of your enduring storms, and past life pain

You are the rain falling on my pain
Nourishing my flower
Assisting it to sprout out of this contaminated soil
While you wash away all of my stains

You are my song that could never go wrong
My melodized notes
Of the words that I quote

A Mothers Need

Instilling in me many strengths and qualities
Your unique love is what I carry
That completely empowers and embody me

Although you had needs
You still planted your seeds
And with that I'll forever be grateful for this woman you produced

With GOD instructions I proclaim that all those broken spirits are loosed
And a newly mature reformed woman is introduced

"A Mothers Need"

Inspired by Christine McGhee

The Main Ingredient

The main ingredient comes from our almighty source
Please trust and believe youll have no remorse
Only a greater sense of direction
An heightened increase of love an affection
As we strive towards Gods perfect will of perfection

Of which increasingly transforms
Ascending us to heightened limits of our regular norm
Carrying us throughout our life journey and storms

The main ingredient is what helps us conform to a wholesome holier life
Enabling us to stand firm through our tests and strife

Contributing to our perseverance
Its a vital necessity of nutrition for our daily consumption
Replenishing and fortifying for our every bodily function

Its an ingredient that we all must consume
Because with the lack of it we are destined to be doomed

So blow on your trumpet and signal the alarm
With Gods perfect first love we are protected from any harm

Spread his infinite word
It continuously travels and remains to be heard

From era to era
Its life sustaining and prosperity framing

The main ingredient that will peacefully calm the soul
Heal the body and restore what the enemy has stole
Then revelations will begin to unfold

While harmonious angel whispers will ring throughout your ear
And the golden lamp of divine light will direct and guide your feet
Through your darkest valleys Gods supernatural powers is what you
will consolingly meet

A heart filled with driven determination through any situation
Full of motivation
Sparked by a fresh salvation
Inevitably embarking us on new brighter unfamiliar destinations

The main ingredient is the salt we need when there is no taste
Inside a lost soul running wild
We use it to tenderize our meat just consider it as the baste

"G"

True love holds the master key to my heart
It was based on your every action and word from the initial start

It helps me to determine if your my man and Im your woman
And if our connection is really suitable

While the both of us deserve and have been longing for a true love thats irremovable

Stable and firm
Like those perfect words of a love song

And not to serve as one of our convenient outlets or voids
Or even be miss-used as available toys

Your love has been contributing to all my strengths
Its not unhealthy or abrusive or causing me any bruising imprints

Its conducively wholesome aiding to the nourishment of my health
Compelling me to remove my "In love" card from off of the shelf

Its administering to me ecstasy
Its extracting out the best in me
An effective antidote that replenishes the less of me

Your love is stimulating and fell in perfect timing
Because this wasteland earthly time is not waiting nor buying

Its cultivating visions of life prosperity in and out my mind
You desirously surpass any of my pass kind
With a certain distinguished quality
Making me curiously eager to collide our souls together and bind
Your love restricts me from any other options

Securely Im leashed to you shackled and chained
All because of your love for me that you managed to maintain

So Im holding on to you
And theres nothing or no one that can undo

So come on enter into my world
Im surely claiming to be only your girl

Im willingly surrendering only to you
Open to share my eternal unique love that can stand throughout the
test of times

That only one woman like me can give
Thats loyal and continually grows and shows all of the days that we live

So let me extinguish you with a dose of this exotic
Providing you my type of perfect hypnotic

Putting you in a pukkin trance
So we could do our love dance

Blending us together as one in unification
As we both explore another romance chance

Inspired by G-Boy

34

"Prize winner"

I feel like Im a prize winner rewarded with a trophy for receiving two lives
Defeating the enemies competition
Overcoming my strongholds and getting presented these divine wings to fly

Saved by grace he granted me immunity to soar
Im highly favored and priviledged to have this opportunity to step through his welcoming door

In my deficiency of lack I carried the cross on my back
My advantage was a wealthy powerful driven spirit
That provided me with the power to persevere on through the totality of all that

My calamities of life is no longer a struggle or fight
All of my counterinfluences can no longer inflict me with strife

Ive been initiated into the gang of conquerors
So vengeance is not what I produce
My heavenly father now contends all of my battles
His undescribable peace to me is what he has introduced

The peace of no ones understanding is what he's been branding
Salvation all across this world is what his descending deliverance is landing

"Master Piece"

After my temple was pulverized I found myself weak
Sifting through my ruins
Salvaging the retrievable broken pieces
As I manage to stand to my feet

Placing them all in a stack
Collecting and putting them in a heavy sack
That Im attempting to carry relentlessly back up this slippery slope on
my back

Now determined and ascending away from my darkest lowered levels
Im climbing into a brighter light
With revisions of greater sight
Avoiding all the hindering evil spirit devils that use to tempt me in my
past life

Finally reaching the slippery slope peak
Through perseverance Ive ascended out of my grave into a new body
and Im no longer weak
Death to life is what I speak
A greater daily intimate connection with GOD is what I greet

My main nourishment of assistance
That supports me to steadfastly stand firm on my feet

As I effortlessly assemble my broken pieces back together
Building from my past testimonial thesis
Equipt with the knowledge Ive obtained throughout my valley journey
Would also contribute to my display of my masterpiece completeness

"Inner Child"

My inner child seems to appear when Im stunned by fear and my
circumstances turn cold
Even though Im an adult shes still an infant incubated hidden deep
inside my soul
When the weight of life pressure gets to heavy to bare
And my vigiliant eyes transform into blinded vision and Im no longer
aware

When Im blindsided and hurt
When my love ones avert

The innocent child awakens with unrecognizable worth
Feeble, searching for any consoling outlet to divert
Her speech had froze when uncomfortability arose

When desecration debilitated our character
The spiritual nourishment of GOD was administered
Then exhilaration stimulated a fresh narrator

Shes just an ordinary ageless undeveloped child
And its been quite a while since Ive seen her smile

Camouflaged beneath my surface
Shes vicariously living through my skin for a purpose

"Colors"

Red is for the bloody trauma leaking out of the laceration deep embedded wounds
From the physical, verbal and emotional abuse
When corrupting evil was introduced to the youths

Black is for the empty vacancies of the voids and needs
When no one was prompted to plant any of their available nourishing seeds

Blue & Purple is for the bruises and blemishes from the damages that permeated their being
Dampening their beauty
Depriving them of the ability to perceive their authentic reflection in the mirror
Distorting their view from seeing

Gray is for the constant shady cloud hovering over their smiles
From the continual contention and neglect
Privy to all the hidden situations that were secretly swept under the deck
When attention and affection was all their innocent souls were set to expect

Yellow is for the bright warm sunshine that crept in drying up their fears
When the smoky elevated dysfunction reeked

And they sat confined in their bedrooms alone staring out the closed
smutty window
And the inundated tears flooded their cheeks
Simmering in the summers heat

Green is for their hope
The paradise visions of their dreams
Euphoric feeling, Toxic free,
Sober and clean from the noxious environment

Pure Fresh Lean engulfed with pasture scenes
Grazing as the flock of sheep
Allowing the shepard to induce their strengths and guide their feet

"Leave me alone"

When I close my eyes I can still envision your face and feel your touch

Its moments like this when I wish I didnt love you that much
Id wish to reject these emotions
But cant help but feel and accept these emotions
You got me intoxicated looking dumb
When my sole reason for the toxic consumptions were only for my feeling to be numbed

I dont want to feel
I dont want to continue to pop these pills
But you still seem to creep in and consume my mind
Someone please instruct me on how to reset and go back and undo our preliminary meeting time

When entangled love transformed into a toxic clot
Congesting both of our hearts
Resulting in our joyous rhythmic beats to stop

Pollution invaded our world
Then trust cultivated into a major factor after I caught you in in bed with that girl

You always promised me that infidelity was not in your nature
But your disloyal actions has motivated my feeling of hatred

So now Im contacting divorce lawyers hunting you down
Singing Usher Raymond Ready for you to sign them papers
As all the rumors spreadabout us all over this town
Now Im the one to blame being accused for putting you down

But Fxxk what they say
Because their not the ones having to walk around displaying these frowns

My heart continuously rips and get torn to pieces
Although the additive of pain has been building to the compilation of my emotional thesis

Drawn from the heartache of pain
Afflicted thoughts from the anguish applied to the brain
Not to mention the elated euphoric feeling from our love that I attempted to maintain

I wish we never met at all
I wish I never accepted your contact information
Leaving you a message then answering your returning call

My mind is completely made up
So when the messenger finds you just sign those papers our time is up

"Leave me alone"

Love Trapped

I feel like these walls strapped
Holding me at gunpoint kidnapped
Isolated behind steele gates
In a designated area up north on the map

Got me expressing my bundled up love to my family on the phone and
through the mail
Reflections of me thinking how did I ever even make it inside this jail
On a crime so intense that I couldnt afford the bail

With only emotions & thoughts I lay trapped in a cell awaiting my
release
My accomplished accumulated certificates and letters sent out to my
judge is my written speech that I preached

Proving to the courts that Im human and made a mistake
A bad choice but now reformed a changed woman thats serving her time
Praying that my crime doesnt stick or define
Hindering any of my future establishments
Obstructing me from reaching out and achieving what is mine

My love can only flow so far in this confined space
Feeling like Im on the sideline sitting stagnant
Disqualified out of my journey race

Nevertheless my heart still beats and my blood is at a steady flow
The lively beats enables me to unclutch my trapped love
Extend it to these foreign acquaintances
That closely reside with me locked behind these closed doors

"Victim to Victor"

Sunk, sitting in my lowest pit after the declension of my downward
spiral in life.
I thought it was over. I thought I was dead
Defeated and disqualified
While remnants of trauma afloat throughout my head
But now ahead
And fully understanding that it was all meant for my ruins
So I could be demolished, renovated and rebuilt
With overcoming, conquering strengths
To be able to with stand any future overwhelming events
To release the weight of any sankers
Those perilous heavy weighted anchors

The reconstruction was right on time, I was right on schedule
I had been saved
Ascended out of my grave
Same face new body restored from the fountain of life
Anointed and equipped, lifted by Christ
Beauty for ashes is what Ive been given
My broken pieces that once blew in the wind was collected and returned
Now my new identity has become my new best friend
Reframed into a master piece
Not knowing that my adversity would lead me to my growth and
achievements.
The chains in my captivity had cultivated various strengths

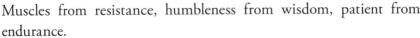

Muscles from resistance, humbleness from wisdom, patient from endurance.
Presenting me a robust body of armour
Prepared for any battle

Moreless vunerable and naive
With revealed abilities to achieve
Anything that my mind is set to.
Aware and on alert for temptations and attacks
That the enemy sends to distract
Transparently able to detect any invitation to deceive
And yes, I have to continuously stay on my knees
Surviving victim to victor is what I have transformed and risen to be.

"Goals"

Goals are chosen roads leading to our accomplishments
They can be big or small
Working towards them gradually brings elevation to all.

Setting them provides us purpose
Instilling worth in us
Leading us to believe
As our action proceeds
We will then achieve
And successful progression will visually be seen.

Allieviating our strife
And instantaneously producing in us life.

"The River That Runs"

The heavenly river that runs consistently with its pleasant tranquilizing flow.
Furnishing my soul with contentment.
Anointing my body from head to toe.
The splashing waves are the whispers of God's infinite word.
That travels worldwide from era to era across every nation to be heard.
It's sustaining nourishment for my life.
Guidance throughout my valley darkest nights.
Encouraging me to keep on abiding in his word.
And continue on to spread what's been heard.
All of your promises has been fullfilling enough to lead this earthly herd.
Convincing me to fully commit and praise you for the rest of my days.
Surfing on the waves of your will depending on them to keep me afloat.
Similar to the protection you placed on Noah's boat.
So let it rain propelling the waves to roar and soar.
Ascending the river banks to higher grounds rising us to greater levels.
While we overcome our hindering devils.
Those precious sounds.
That the thunder rings down.
Signaling for our attention.
Like the visibly unyielded red flags the blind eye could not recognize.
But you mercifully still cradle us in the palm of your hands.
Assisting us to avoid that obstructing enemy.
Contributing to our fortitude allowing us to stand.

48

And as the water streams persistently throughout this land.

We conquer enslaved oppression.

With frequent absorption it eliminates desperation.

Revealing within us fresh unfamiliar strengths, gifts and talents to explore.

Healing and restoring.

Sailing our stray boats back up to shore.

Walking us into new opportunities, opening doors.

Which will remarkably produce within us higher scores.

The never ending river that you can never ignore.

It abundantly runs and consuming it makes life worth its rapid run.

"You Made Me New"

You made me new like you created the heavens and earth
Commanding "Let there be light"
Separating me from my darkness breathing into me new life
With out you 'O Lord I could have not seen it any other way
You've opened my mind up to visualize many new perspectives
Things are much more friendlier and brighter each day
Once blind and not noticing that you've been right by my side every
step of the way
Throughout all of my days
Although I was falling and rising I grew weary at times
My faith was being stretched, bent, crushed as my circumstances fell
apart over times
Though I had fallen and sat in darkness
You promised I will rise again
The Lord is my light and He will transit me on into new light
Diverting me away from this secular world of sin
Your bread has unsealed me, You made me new
Your consecration has set me apart
Providing me this fresh restart
Equipping me with provision, fortitude and tenacity as I am reformed
Now aware of the lessons and gifts that you have administered to me
throughout all of my storms
Ive endured the resistance of my journey
But with resiliency Ive overcame
Developing powerful new strengths of self-discipline and control

With new profound salvation and by me consistently praising your name

Gaining a better sense of direction and exploring new routes

Rebuilding and resetting my ruins has been my present guidance putting God first with no doubts

Once blind but know seeing, Im stepping into this new being

Transparently navigating through this time

Flying free with the angels and so elated to have committed to make you mine

YOU MADE ME NEW "IM FREE"

And who the son sets free is free indeed

Your sufficient for all no matter our falls

And you are a God that will supply our every needs

"Greater Is Coming"

Greater is coming are the words I've been given
I'm totally lifted and encouraged as I walk boldly throughout this prison
Standing grounded in the light God is assisting me to stand
Revealing to me fresh profound abilities I no longer settle on the enemies land

Im following your imprinted footprints you left visible in the sand
O precious almighty Lord creator of all please continue to keep a tight grip of my hand
Im listening trusting and believing in you as JOB did
Enduring all my lessons tests
Throughout my valley and when Im face down in my mess
Dreaming and expecting my futures best
Because you promised in my latter days my best is still yet to come
Noticing that the more intimate we get
The more clearer my perspectives and actions will shift
Although no matter my past infirmaties your a God that never takes score
Your grace and mercy is beautifully renewed each day
So you could never ignore
You sit patiently awaiting with open arms for us to walk through that everlastingly open heavenly door

Departing from my old body and comfortably stepping into the new
God is the solution to our life friction

And the complete draping of our benedictions
Close to you Im acquiring a peaceful stable understanding as I persistently pursue
A GREATER IS COMING
And thats all Im wanting to convey to you

"Green Light"

My source gave me the light said it was green so go
Hesitant at the initial start
But now Im equipt and even more ready to blossom and flow
With a sober diverse mindset that has broadened to conceive
And convey my life journey and all of my formulated ideas that's
compressed inside of me
My dreams and goals were once thrown away
Im on a fresh route now after relentlessly trying
My soul back then was slowing dying
Now decompressing in this jail cell has been my new therapeutic finding
A present gift revealed in my darkest pits
Releasing my thoughts taking the weight off my brain
An essential positive toxic free outlet thats assisting to keep my mental
ability sane
And free from the present circumstances of my pain
And strife while the clock is winding down on my life
The enemy strategy was to corrupt and dismantle me
My mistakes the voices and all the wrong choices in my life
A direct motive to unable me to hear or see what God has woven me
to be
So I had to sit still and self-examine the remnants of my choices
Consider all consequences and open up my mind to new perspectives
And listen to those heavenly voices
Taking a detour and coming out of it all
With Gods shedding light Im still standing tall

Because it was not of me only what I could see
Only what my culture trauma and pain had shaped and molded me to be
You got the "GREEN LIGHT" go you are finally set free
A reset has begun
My soul is refreshed like the new day of the rising morning sun
Overcoming what once was and discovering my true value
An unfamiliar revealed element Ive obtained throughout my travel
I can now recognize more purpose from a positive direction
Now looking in the mirror at a more transparent reflection
No more tears or fears only acceptance and stride
Im expanding my visions and hope while pursuing this new path of my life
Recognizing that God has always been right by my side
Whispering "GREEN LIGHT" go your no longer blind
Now see my child this faith and salvation is what I have been trying to reveal to you your entire lifetime

Your now free

"Innocent Seeds"

Their presence, their lives, their love are my true blessing sent from
God above
They are the reactants that ignite the beats of my heart
Transporting the blood from my heart throughout my body
When they initially inhaled their first breaths from the start

My innocent seeds, the productions from my births
My pure introductions to this earth
Gods beautiful perfectly woven creations
Withholding so much precious worth

Birthed into this world of sin
Helpless and chosen to be apart of my life pressure of strain
Wearing a smile so bright
Innocent and blind to any of this worldly pain

Just know that you have been the aid to my strength and motivation
Restricting me from getting lost further in my wilderness of hopeless
desperation
My loves, my breed, my innocent seeds
Who unfortunately became cultivated into damaged fruit
From the noxious exposure of my actions and roots

Now abandoned walking throughout your own life journey alone

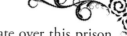

My perception of what Im receiving as we conversate over this prison phone
Searching and roaming to now fill your voids and needs
Im incarcerated, daily praying for your protection and peace getting down on bended knees
Visualizing these generational cursed cycles
Simultaneously mentalizing the negative dysfunction thats being so routinely recycled

Destiny
Dynasty
Michael
Misan

"You Cant Win With Sin"

We cannot win with the presence of sin
Without surrendering to Gods will
And the ceasing of our own will that blows continuously in the wind
Without the light that guides and overrides the dark nights
Provided from our most powerful force our source "GOD"
He is the ultimate nourishment the fertilizer of our souls
Our deepest private secrets he holds

Hes the unearther of our weeds
The planter of our seeds
The spirit that rains upon them cultivating a bountiful harvest that
supply our every needs

With sin we are unable to win and our lives decline
As we deprive ourselves an continue to walk as the blind
Obstructed from the light of clear sight
Blocking the true meaning of Gods purpose and plans for our life
We cannot when without the "Shedding of our skin"
Our testimony that rebuilds our crushing and trials
Our endurance of life miles
Or the pride of life that puts us all to the test
Similar to the lusting of our flesh
The idolizing of these earthly material possessions
When we should be valuing every God given blessing

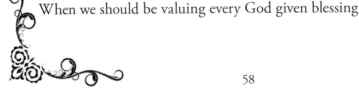

The substances thats of greater significance quality and worth is what Im confessing

We cannot win without the unification of our diverse soul being
Overcoming and understanding our uniqueness
Like the variations of our skin our cultures our sculptures that shape
build and mold us into our own distinctive being

How can we win?

"Street Life"

Street life is where alot of lost souls coast
Residing in noxious environments
Running day and night throughout the calendar days doing the most

Making several uncontemplated choices
Succumbing to the enemies evil voices
We got the drug afflictions
From the variety of embedded addictions
Whether its hustling or using
They both equally leave you in contention positions.

Although daily death is lurking around the corner at your neck.
They refuse to try something different
Like laboring an honest 9 to 5 to legally receive a check.

Armed with guns
Surrounding themselves with harm
They still feel its the most intellectual way.
Living by those four words "By any means necessary" Im'a collect
that pay.

Screaming wheres the smoke because we want more
Theres them gangsta arrested developement soldiers shaped and molded
ready for war.

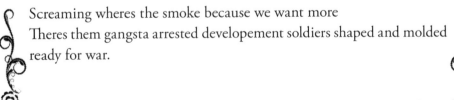

The human bodies continue to be slain
Families left with only memories
Suffering from the blood stains.
Leading us to think was our precious childbirths of life all in vain.
As we awake in our deepest, darkest pits
Our vision is made clear after the light hits
The sanity of it all was it worth the waste
Jumping on that slippery slope of the street life which inevitably leads to our fall
Now unfortunately were out of this life race with no existence at all

"Bullet Magnets"

Bullet magnets are the banged out gangs flagged out in our communities
Contending to fight over colors and turf
But when will they get to recognize their true meaning of a full life worth
Instead they proceed on to kill one another robbing our mothers of their precious childbirths
Their getting body bagged packed off for buriels riding away in a hearst
A young mankind gone in a nick of time
Not even getting the chance to experience the true meaning of a full lifetime

Bullet magnets are also of African American descent
Theres ongoing police brutality no matter the event
Because as of today our justice system is still bent
Obstructing our freedom and hindering our abilities to evolve
Martin Luther King stated "We shall overcome"
But the remaining issue have still yet to be resolved

Bullet magnets are those hoodstars battling over clout
And pushing drugs to survive
Engaging into criminal activities to provide
Wearing written targets on their backs
Blood Lust and money in the oppositions eyes they attract

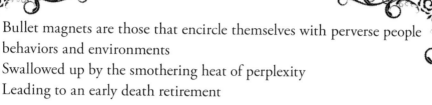

Bullet magnets are those that encircle themselves with perverse people
behaviors and environments
Swallowed up by the smothering heat of perplexity
Leading to an early death retirement

BULLET MAGNETS BODIES CONSUMED WITH HOT METAL
FRAGMENTS

"Gang Involvement"

THE GANG INVOLVEMENT MAKES ME QUESTION
DO WE DO IT FOR THE FAME
OR IS IT THAT APPEALING TO US TO BE RECOGNIZED BY
CREATING A NEGATIVE NAME

WHEN ALL THE SENSELESS VIOLENCE BODIES DROP
WHO DO WE REALLY NEED TO BLAME
OUR MIS-LED, MIS-GUIDED FATHERLESS FIGURES, ITS A
SHAME
NOW THE STATISTICS ARE GROWING AND SHOWING
MEN BEHIND BARS WITH #'S REPLACING THEIR BIRTH
NAMES

IM TRYING TO CHANGE PERSPECTIVES
TO VISUALIZE, DREAM & REACH TOWARDS LEGIT
BUSINESSES AS OUR NEW ELECTIVES
TO MAKE OUR PRESENT DAILY CHOICES SELECTIVE

SETTING EXAMPLES THAT WILL MATTER
SO OUR UPCOMING GENERATIONAL CYCLE WILL EXCELL
IN THE LATTER

TO START TRENDING
LIVING LIFE FOR A PURPOSE AND A REASON
AND NOT FOR JUST A MEANINGLESS SEASON

Gang Involvement

"Emotional Thug"

Emotional thug in need of love
Just consider me an hood angel thats heaven sent from up above
I can relate to your grind and mind
Bring backbone support to the spine
A listening ear
As we unwind I'll give you my undivided attention over a glass of wine
I'm absorbing all of your pain
Your venting telling me that you feel like your life journey has all been
in vain
Raised in the south
Growing up with both parents holding crack pipes in their mouths
So with no sense of guidance
You were marked with defiance
Opposing to all the rules
You dropped out of school
Living life in the streets pushing drugs toting tools
On the outside looking in its all toughness you seem cool
But up close and in intimate relations
I see that thugs really require love too
Its alright go ahead and cry
Thats what all humans are created to do
Liberate the pain, Try and remain sane
Im only here to console and assist you through this strain
To help you regain focus and alleviate the weight off your brain
So you dont have to self-medicate and stay lit

Honey listen let me tell you
Where you at and the way you living isnt it
God has created us all with a plan
So withdraw from the enemy sought suicidal thoughts
Not giving in letting them take its stand
Speak life into every situation, You are gonna live
God will eventually restore
Filling all your empty voids and needs abundantly providing you with more
Just pray and pay close attention start listen
Because you are one of his children that he adores

A Better Place Now

Im in a better place now since youve entered my space
Im totally convinced that Im here to stay
Floating once again on another cloud with untamed heart vibrations
paving the way
Just when I thought strategic steele barriers were planted and
Stood in place
Like a robber committing a heist in the night
You trespassed over the gates in my captivity
Sharing your goals and kidnapping my soul

Telling me your here to stay
Connecting and building with me day to day

Im in a better place now your my comfort in my distress
Solace is what I hold even though my emotions are on a high running
outta control
Yes I want to surrender to this heart of gold
Aware of both of our past
I understand that sometimes fairytales do unfold
Is this present vision of us a chapter of my life that needs to be told
We hold a multitude of commonalities that'll perfectly mesh
Your discourse your actions are passing all of my tests
Rewind the resurfaced emotions let the love lead the way
Cultivate the good energy and smiles
As I awake it paints my face throughout the day

Im in a better place now your welcomed so come on in
Im open and willing to blossom from more than just friends
You say youve always held me close in your heart

Thats why this unexpected start never displayed any doubt
Your rewiring my brain future feeling of so much gain
Sending numbing transmitters over all of my heavy weighted pain

Just some of life simple fun
While off to the races were jumping the gun

Were in a better place now both you and me
So elevating
Directly in the comfort of your arms is where Im wanting to be

Continue to reach for this star in the night that still shines bright
Providing me a reason for our season
Provoking me to share my light
So tell me teach me of all that you desire
My boundless loyalty and security will surely inspire
With limitless love that overflows and fills the soul
So get a tighter grip of my cup and position a better hold

Here in a better place now

"Fast Food Franchise"

Young motionless fallen souls
Bloody bodies layed out across every restaurant franchise floor.

As the contacted families gather and sit at bay
The emergency units work effectively to resuscitate
The victims family trys to cope
Then they soon relate to similar previous senseless crimes
As their trauma resonates.

So many senseless deaths are filling our families plates
While flying bullets keep meeting and greeting us on blind dinner dates.

I suggest we visit Gods venue
And see whats appetizing on that menue.
Because so many orders are getting dropped
When will this repetitive cycle of violence be put to a stop.

In the kitchen is where our main ingredient is always burning.
On a platter prepared and ready to serve the ultimate nourishment of food.
That our soul is everlastingly yearning.

We need to order more "CHRIST" To feed more life.

"Mature Intimate Connections"

My will refuses to eat off your dollars or grind
Because my mind is independently mentally empowered
Fully focused with abilities to jump onto any selected avenue of revenue
To reach out and grab mines
Just feed me the proper attention, your mind and time
And beautifully our souls will collide together and everything will be just fine

Let me learn and determine your movements when your consumed with the smoke
When life gets bad your frustrated and broke
Let me experience your actions when your glad sad or mad
Let me see how you respond to the step kids when they start to call you dad

Get acquainted with my soul
Without any of your tangible insertions being applied to my holes
Or even before you have any intentions on invading my bodies mold

Ill prefer the mental intercourse any day because its much more pleasing
Compared to the sexual intercourse thats less complex but much more easy

Penetrate me spiritually allowing your soul to collide with mines
So you could dwell inside my temple & reside with me over these times

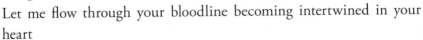

Let me flow through your bloodline becoming intertwined in your heart
Merging deep within your DNA so scientifically we could never be apart

Its exciting while our amplified heightened upgraded emotions are spiritually uniting
Making it all worth the effort
As sweet visions travel amongst our thoughts
Leading us to an island of suspense anticipating the special moments of our upcoming events
Every hour provide me power setting the perfect solid foundation
As we continue to stack our love as high as the Iffle Tower
Settling on a high rise as we grow older
Shoulder to shoulder
Reminiscing about our past
With unbreakable ties that will foreverly be built to last

"You Love Me You Want Me"

You love me you want me
Then you ask me not to crush you
I suppose only trust you
And immediately open up my heavenly love gates
Before weve had any dates

You love me you want me
Then dont place me in your mind as a hurricane
Thats here to administer to you a worldwind of pain
While we both are in pursuit to be one anothers main

Fully understand that Im not that type
Im just a ghetto angel in need of a real man in my life to handle me right
My roots are unique and of distinctive brand
A kind that you may have never experienced in your life plan or uprooted
off this land
Im not present in your life to take this time for granted
What we have began to plant has already been planted
Im not here to make you cry or fall
Or to tell you any childish immature lies at all

Honesty is always what I speak and convey
And all my daily actions will soon display

Love me Want me
Because we both obtained a gain
Of mutual feeling between two mutual being seeing mutual seeing
Uniting and taking mutual risks
On a mission hoping for an eternity of completeness
And love that will forever remain in our mists

You Love Me You Want Me

"When Love Hurts"

Whats the value of trust when its consistently breakable through lust
When all self-discipline and control gets lost
In the tangible fluid touches of the other people sauce
Damaging the mutual feeling of what was thought to be in our hearts
Tearing us both apart
Crumbling all of the verbalized vows that were spoken at the initial start
Altering moods, returning our spectacular smiles back into voided frowns
As the sound of our rapid heart rate elevates with its irregular pounds
Just then our floating proud spirits will suddenly descend from the elation clouds settling closer to the ground
Simmering idle from its heightened emotional states
Of the two compassionate coupling mates
Due to the impact of the couples hurt
It has lessened the elevated loves worth
Undoing the intertwined grasps of the hands
Propelling us towards another stance
Shifting our positioned feet that once stood so solid together on our built foundation of land
Is this zealous burst of love
Worth all the indepths hurt of love
When Love Hurts
We can count it all joy and foreverly remain grateful & in acceptance
Living in contentment with the painless purified first love
Administered only from our main source, the one & only God above

"How Am I Suppose To Love Again"

We displayed smiles, Tied lifetime vows
How am I suppose to love again
When my soul is still carrying around all these empty holes in them
At a certain point of time we both conceived thoughts of being lifetime
friends
Ive always stood right by your side ten toes down even when my broken
heart had to mend
MARY J BLIGE stay down
As your disloyal tail ran so freely around this town
I stayed down through whatever I had your back
I'd hit them tracks
And when I had to I'd tote the strap
Without any questions I will gladly oblige and do just that
I loved you only
TONI BRAXTON how many ways
I had insanely committed to be your personal slave
It was suppose to be us side by side throughout all of our days
Let me count the ways
Because I carried the majority of the weight
Placing no one above you
When your currency came in late
My supernatural love is what kept us during those dates
In addition to the provided food that I placed on our plates
I conceived all your children
Upfront and honest with you always letting you know what Im doing

You knew of my every movements
Never missing a beat
And as our romantic melody played in my mind we were grooving
But you were still unsatisfied on the outside lusting and ???
Intuitively I knew what you were doing RAY J. if I had one wish
I would wish I hadnt took that chance
Allowing you up in my space filling that position to be my man
Rearranging my steps wishing to recast my past times
Maybe then I wouldnt be sitting here in my feeling writing down these ill rhymes
HOW CAN I LOVE AGAIN?
With the combined companionship of two souls again
How can I fill these voided vacant holes within
After I have given you the best of me
Crossing every ocean and the multitude of seas
While the incomplete love you was given was only what my naive perceived eyes could see
I just want relations to let me be
No restraints, no expectations or any warranted unexpected hurt
No excuses no complaints!!!
Just me alone loving me flying free doing me

"Fall"

Heading into the month of December
Looking out of my window at the end of November
Theres the barely naked brittle trees
With only a few remaining dangling orange and brown blended fall colored leaves
What a delightful sight
The season of the raging sun has dimmed its lights
Now the sky is visibly seen more somber
As the cool wind incites the branches motioning them from left to right
Similar to the waving hand
Welcoming and anticipating the upcoming snowfall thats soon to drizzle across the land
And as all the chirping black birds gather
They form their herd and prepare to fly south following directives from their leading commander
While the mother bird stuff worms in the young chicks mouth

Once again the pedestrians dress attire will alter
Due to the frigid temperatures
Stepping outside no one really wants to bother

Events will begin to be delayed
And the outside tone will become much softer
Everyone seem to be in good cheer
These times are the most memorable moments of the year
Because of Thanksgiving holiday and Jesus Christ birthdate is near.

"Escape"

If I could I would run off into the woods getting lost in the wilderness.
Naked and free like Adam and Eve
To evade all of the evil and bitterness that has incorporated this world.
Due to the lost manskind of the boy and girl

I would run so long until the night falls
Lay out in the grass under the tall trees
And just gaze at the stars.
While the cluster of biting insects mingle and put on their show
I'd listen to the whispers of the cold wind that blows
Vocalizing the foreign language that comes from our creator
Instilling the peace and contentment
Stating our days will become greater later
Appearing out of their homes
The wild animals freely roam
Perfering the night rather than day
While the viscous alligators sit by the river front at bay
On alert, patiently awaiting on something to devour as their prey.
Its the ultimate tranquility
Feeling like a relaxant pill is in me
No emotions or mental storms
O'Lord how I wish this could be my real life norm.

But its only my imaginated fiction
In hope to stimulate your mental and give a description
Of a way I can trigger your mind to relate
To my formulated diverse freeways of thoughts of my escape.

Hood Love

The beauty of it all is that we both can relate in more ways than one
By being sincerely honest mature and genuine with love contemplating
on whats next to come
Despite of our separate journeys weve been handling one another with
encouragement consolation compassion and care
From the hope of our broken pieces
Revealing all nakedness
With no opinions or prejudgements just bare

Hood love that is what this season has sparked
Just let the flames remain to burn its been our light in the dark

Hood love inspires the both of us
We are familiar with our roots understanding our truths
So comfort and understanding wont carry any contention under our
roof

Just a simple unique connection a blessing
Complimenting one another as we gaze in each other eyes
As if were looking into a mirror with similar reflections

You of me and me of you pushing towards the mark of a higher calling
of what hood love has compelled us to see

Planting seeds for our harvest and praying that our source send the rain
Ascending us beyond our roadblocks and circumstances feeling no pain

Displaying determination and faith while navigating through the unknown
Eagerly and certain that we will see this fantasy through until I can return back home

An angel God has sent in my darkest valley can it be true
Compatibly recognizing and understanding the true blue
Im just gonna let the process cultivate the strengths into an unbreakable force HoodLove"
Who would of knew

Building a foundation then a homes
Leading us to our thrones
Come a little closer baby Im on my way home

Idle confinement

Incarceration solitude
Eyeballs clocking my every move as if I were nude
Surveillance on me 24/7
The verbage on my tongue are my repents and wishes that are sent up
daily to heaven

Idled, confined, content in my cell
With drawn from the prison crowd in my own Lil bubble
Away out of everyone elses proximity avoiding the loud noise
And any of the unnecessary noxious trouble.

My silent idle space is where the angels voices whisper
My intimate moments with God
My sacred heavenly prayer communication zone
Where only me and my emotions and thoughts would roam
Where I can drift off to distant euphoric destinations an conceive
nostalgia memories of home

Its where my heart is fenced around hurt
And my tear ducts are profusely flowing inundated with water gushing
forth spurts
Cleaning my soul extracting out my past dirt

Its where Gods light illuminated my darkness
Bringing forth immense unfamiliar revelations

A place where Ive learned to lean solely on a more in depth relation with my salvation

Its where a fresh identity has been birthed
And I am now recognizing and considering my worth
After discerning that all my past unhealthy relationships were cursed

Its where Im maturing in my pain
As I simmer in the boiling rain of my valley storms
Ironically its conducively contributing to my vitality

Im in solitude confinement
But what I discovered and dug up was a diamond

A substance carrying a tremendous amount of value
Fine quality
Dusted off and refined
Exceptionally equipped
Polished and ready to shine

The Penal System

Through the penal system Ive had the privilege to experience both sides
An advantage over my past
Grateful that my heart still beats
And Im still standing breathing alive

I send up the praises to my higher power for the mercy he has given
And his resurrected rebirth of an awakened revised citizen
Its like Ive been blessed and gifted with two lives

The penal system is chastising my character defects
Inseminating in me reconstructive effects
While eradicating my dampening emotions of a rejects

Its enhancing my entire being
As I audaciously navigate through fresh beginning of greater envisioned scenes

Resetting my morals to heightened levels
As I walk towards open opportunist doors
An uncomfortable space that I would usually bypass and ignore

This is an embracing whipping that I would never forget
The type of nourishing well needed planted tools preparing me to be fully equipt

Impacting, Reflecting
Consumed with bitter sweet emotions
But Im sanguinely collecting all of the tokens
The sweet deposits into the chosen

Its been the catalyst of the 'Shedding of my Skin"
The humanizing of my restraint voice
As my muscles cultivate through resiliency from the pressure weight of
life turbulent wind

It has me calculating my goals
Paving the path for my future roads
Ultimately driven by my spiritual soul
Facilitating my growth and relinquishing the corrupting hindering
mold of the old

The penal system providing me with the tools to fearlessly uproot my
past
And while sifting through my dirt I discovered a golden promising
identity thats robustly built to last

"Deface"

Shaped like a coke bottle
With a waist line resembling a slender model
Shes defecting Gods fearlessly wonderfull woven creation
With artificial deposits implanted to enhance her exterior location
Not fully apprehensive of her true worth
She feels better esteemed with a big booty in a short revealing skirt
with no shirt

The upper portion of her body displayed a tiny bra
And as she ran the streets she developed a degrading name of a renown
promiscuous hood star
Soliciting her body jumping in and out of stranger cars
Mingling with celebrities
Dipping and dabbing into drugs
Exposing her to addiction
Partying drinking flipping through several bars

This undiscovered phenomenal woman didnt make it to far
Until her lifestyle had took her to a remote dark valley
Away from the street life that her upbringing had carved
And after sitting idle in her mess
And turning down all of the noise
She developed a content calmer state of poise

She began to reflect and self evaluate her life
Communicate with God and let him guide her towards his life sustaining light
He gradually eradicated all of her misinformed information
And revealed in her fresh brighter revelations

And in her preservation
His supernatural powers extracted out a new revised creation
Positioning her inside a more pleasant toxic free fulfilling destination
Recognizing her own authentic self value influence and appearance
Deflecting her away from what her past life was steering
Shes been defaced
Bound then found
Replaced with a healthier identity
As of now shes living sound

Epilogue

Once dead in my transgressions and driven by this earthly realm
My eyes couldnt see beyond my flesh
I wasnt receptive to the freely first love my higher power had given me.
The fearlessly wonderful handwork of his creations "My Body"
The washing away and forgiveness of my sins "The Blood"
The mighty grace he has presented to me daily "Mercy"
I was saved through "Faith"
My redeemer had sent me a deposit the "Holy Spirit"
Convicting me and assisting me to stand firm believing in his word
He anointed my head
Providing me with provision, enlightenment and revelations
Something my eyes have never seen or my mind could never grasp
Its the consolation, motivation, hope and empowerment it all brings
To love, inspire and shed light on unclean things
Its the holy influence
Peace and inner increase of life
For a better version of me
To be of service as an instrument for you
To convey his purpose and commands
When all hope is lost and your unwilling to stand
When you stumble in life with feeling of shame, guilt, stress, inadequacy, discouragement and uncertainty
Set your face on God our source
Stay grounded on your spiritual path keeping it in your heart and mind as your first choice

For his word is sufficient for all and can supply our every need
My savior our sovereign father sits high above and showers us with unrecognizable gifts.
His plans are to prosper us and not to harm us
Because he delights in the prosperity of the righteousness
Providing us strengths to conquer any opposition that comes up against us.
Because when we are weak we are strong we are "Overcomers"

Printed in the United States
by Baker & Taylor Publisher Services